GOLD
MEDAL
GAMES

TEAM SPORTS
OF THE
WINTER GAMES

Aaron Derr

RED
CHAIR
·PRESS·

Gold Medal Games is produced and published by Red Chair Press:

Red Chair Press LLC   PO Box 333   South Egremont, MA 01258-0333

www.redchairpress.com

Publisher's Cataloging-In-Publication Data

Names: Derr, Aaron, author. | Sperling, Thomas, 1952- illustrator.

Title: Team sports of the Winter Games / Aaron Derr ; [illustrations by Thomas Sperling].

Description: South Egremont, MA : Red Chair Press, [2020] | Series: Gold medal games | Interest age level: 007-010. | Includes bibliographical references and index. | Summary: "An overview of the modern Olympic Games featuring Winter sports played by teams of athletes competing against each other ... These athletes compete in more than 100 team events. The games showcase the strength and skills, stamina and endurance of amazing athletic teams from around the world in a show of sportsmanship."--Provided by publisher.

Identifiers: ISBN 9781634407236 (library hardcover) | ISBN 9781634407281 (paperback) | ISBN 9781634407335 (ebook)

Subjects: LCSH: Winter Olympics--Juvenile literature. | Team sports--Juvenile literature. | CYAC: Winter Olympics. | Sports.

Classification: LCC GV841.5 .D472 2020 (print) | LCC GV841.5 (ebook) | DDC 796.98--dc23

LCCN: 2018963386

Illustrations by Thomas Sperling.

Photo credits: cover (top), cover (right), pp. 1, 3, 5, 15, 17, 22, 25, 27, 30, 33, 35, 37, 41, 45–47 Shutterstock; cover (left) © ZUMA Press, Inc./Alamy; pp. 6 (top), 31 (top), 34–35, 40 © PA Images/Alamy; pp. 7, 28 Library of Congress; p. 9 © Sueddeutsche Zeitung Photo/Alamy; pp. 12–13 © 615 Collection/Alamy; p. 16 Library and Archives Canada; pp. 23, 38, 39, 43 © Xinhua/Alamy; pp. 24–25, 26 (top, bottom), 33, 42 © dpa picture alliance/Alamy; p. 29 © Keystone Pictures USA/Alamy; p. 31 (bottom) © Sport in Pictures/Alamy; p. 36 © Bygone Collection/Alamy; p. 37 © Andrew Benton/Alamy; p. 4 © B Bennett/ Getty; pp. 6 (bottom), 10 © Topical Press Agency/Alamy; p. 8 © De Agostini Picture Library/Alamy; pp. 11, 14 © Bettmann/Alamy; p. 18 © Sovfoto/Alamy; p. 19–21 © Heinz Kluetmeier/Alamy; p. 32 © Jerry Cooke/Getty Images.

Printed in the United States of America

0619 1P CGS20

TABLE OF CONTENTS

TEAM SPORTS AT THE WINTER GAMES

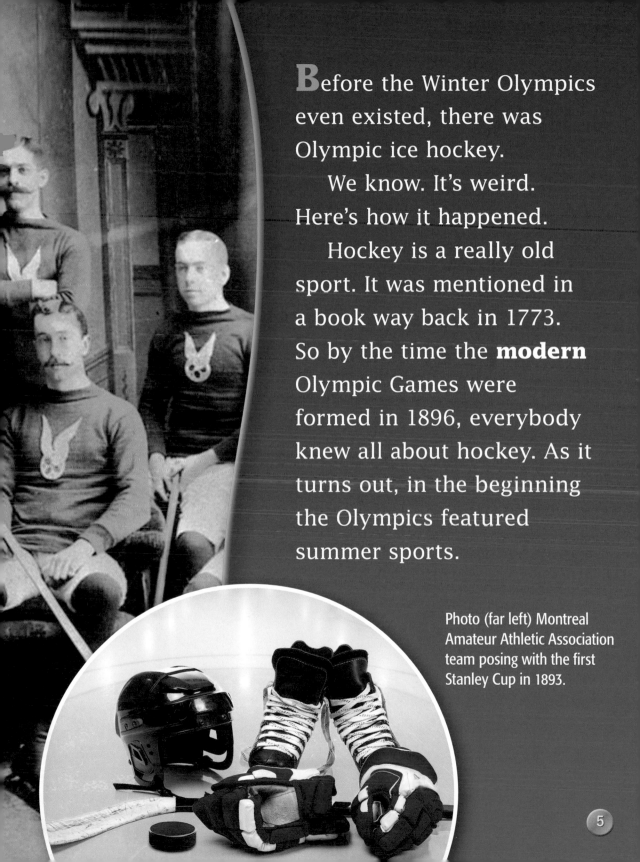

Before the Winter Olympics even existed, there was Olympic ice hockey.

We know. It's weird. Here's how it happened.

Hockey is a really old sport. It was mentioned in a book way back in 1773. So by the time the **modern** Olympic Games were formed in 1896, everybody knew all about hockey. As it turns out, in the beginning the Olympics featured summer sports.

Photo (far left) Montreal Amateur Athletic Association team posing with the first Stanley Cup in 1893.

Figure skating came to the Olympics in the 1908 Summer Olympics. More and more people wanted to see winter sports in the Olympics.

1908 skating gold medalist: Sweden's Ulrich Salchow

Winter sports were popular at the 1908 games in London.

Finally, ice hockey made its Olympic debut in the 1920 Summer Olympics. It was the first winter team sport to be held at the Olympics. In fact, ice hockey was the first event held in the 1920 Games.

The Canadian team was unstoppable. In their first game, they beat Czechoslovakia 15-0. In the next game, they beat the United States 2-0. At least the Americans kept it close! Canada then won the gold medal game 12-1 against Sweden.

Olympic hockey was a hit—fans loved it.

USA hockey team in 1920 Summer Olympics

Shortly after the 1920 Summer Games, it was decided that winter sports would get its own Olympics. The first ever Winter Olympic Games were held in 1924, and hockey has been included ever since.

FYI

The Winter Olympics used to be held the same year as the Summer Olympics. After the 1992 Games, the next Winter Olympics were held in 1994 so they could be held in different years from the Summer Games.

Another winter Olympic team sport is curling. Like hockey, it was included in the 1924 Winter Games. After that, however, it would be a long time before curling made it back to the Olympics as an official event.

Curling was a demonstration sport for the next 74 years. A demonstration sport doesn't count in the final medal standings. They are included to show fans how the sport is played.

It wasn't until 1998 in Nagano that curling was officially an Olympic sport again.

Curling as a demonstration sport, Winter Games, 1936 in Garmisch-Partenkirchen, Germany

Introducing ... Bobsleigh!

The final winter Olympic team sport is bobsled. Officially, it's called bobsleigh, and it requires a team of drivers to **steer** a sled down an icy track. The best bobsleigh teams really fly down the **track**.

Bobsleigh has been an official Winter Olympic sport every year except 1960. For the 1960 Winter Games, **organizers** decided it would be too expensive to build a bobsleigh run. Bobsleigh fans were not happy!

The British bobsleigh team won a Silver medal at the first Winter Olympics, 1924 in Chamonix, France.

The International Bobsleigh and Tobogganing Federation is the group in charge of **international** bobsleigh competition. They begged for the Olympics to **reconsider** their decision.

After much **discussion**, it was decided that the cost of building a bobsleigh run in Squaw Valley, California, just wasn't worth it. To fans' delight, it was the only time in Winter Olympic history that bobsleigh events weren't held.

Mostly, bobsleigh teams have had four people. In 1928, the Olympics used five-man bobsleigh teams. But most international teams used four people, so the Olympics went back to four-person teams after that.

In 1932, they added a two-person bobsleigh race, and that event has continued ever since. In 2002, women were finally allowed to compete in bobsleigh as well.

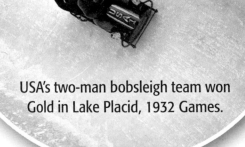

USA's two-man bobsleigh team won Gold in Lake Placid, 1932 Games.

Gold Medal Cities

The Winter Olympics are hosted by a different city every four years.
Here is a list of the host cities for the most recent and future Winter Games.

2026: Milan/Cortina
      d'Ampezzo

2022: Beijing

2018: Pyeongchang

2014: Sochi

2010: Vancouver

2006: Turin

2002: Salt Lake City

1998: Nagano

1994: Lillehammer

1992: Albertville

1988: Calgary

1984: Sarajevo

1980: Lake Placid

1976: Innsbruck

1972: Sapporo

1968: Grenoble

1964: Innsbruck

1960: Squaw Valley

1956: Cortina d'Ampezzo

The Winter Olympics have been held on three different **continents**: North America, Europe and Asia.

CHAPTER 2

HOCKEY

Team Canada wins the Gold
medal for hockey, 1928 in
St. Moritz, Switzerland

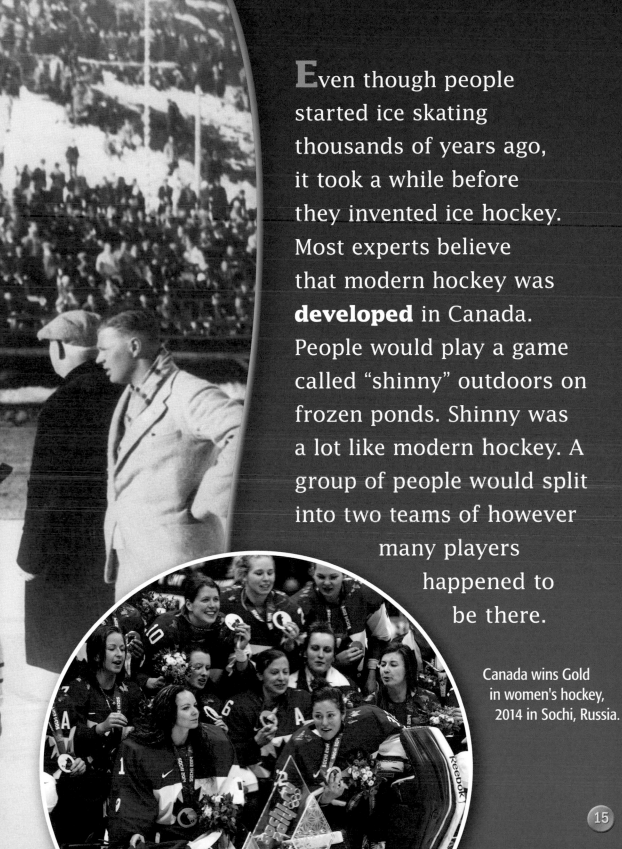

Even though people started ice skating thousands of years ago, it took a while before they invented ice hockey. Most experts believe that modern hockey was **developed** in Canada. People would play a game called "shinny" outdoors on frozen ponds. Shinny was a lot like modern hockey. A group of people would split into two teams of however many players happened to be there.

Canada wins Gold in women's hockey, 2014 in Sochi, Russia.

Instead of using nets for goals, they would just mark the goals with rocks or a big block of snow. And they had a blast playing!

The first official indoor hockey game was played in 1875 in the Canadian town of Montreal. A man named James Creighton had started organizing games of shinny at an indoor ice skating rink. But Creighton added more rules to the game. The rules limited the number of players per team to nine, and they had flags placed 8 feet (2.5 m) apart to mark the goals.

James Creighton

Canadian fans celebrate Men's and Women's gold medals in Sochi, 2014.

A report in the Montreal Gazette newspaper the next day said that "a very large audience" watched the game, and that the spectators were "well satisfied with the evening's entertainment."

Eventually, the number of players per side was reduced from nine to six, including the goalie. But one thing never changed: Canadiens loved hockey. It quickly became the nation's most popular sport!

That's probably why Canada won six of the first seven gold medals awarded in Olympic hockey.

Miracle on Ice

One of the most exciting Olympic hockey games ever played was in the 1980 Games in Lake Placid, New York. The United States was the host team, but they had a big **challenge** ahead of them: the Soviet Union.

The team from the Soviet Union was the defending gold medalist. They had won five of the previous six gold medals at the Winter Olympics. While Canada had **dominated** early Olympic hockey, the Soviet Union was clearly the best team during this time.

The USSR team (Soviet Union) in 1980 seemed unbeatable.

The Miracle on Ice, USA versus USSR,
1980 Winter Games in Lake Pacid.

It didn't seem like the Americans would be able to stop them in 1980. The Soviet team included mostly professional players—some of the best players in the world. The U.S. team was made up of amateur players—young players who didn't have much experience playing against really good teams.

Great Game!

After the first period, the game was tied 2–2. The Soviet Union scored next to take a 3–2 lead, but the United States scored twice in the final period to pull in front 4–3. The crowd was going crazy! They began to **chant**, "USA! USA!"

The Soviets tried to **rally** several times in the final minutes of the game, but the United States held on to win. As time ran out, the television announcer excitedly asked the viewers watching at home, "Do you believe in miracles?"

The American fans in attendance were cheering like mad. And so were people all across the United States who were watching at home. The American team went on to win the gold medal.

"You're looking for players whose name on the front of the sweater is more important than the one on the back," said American coach Herb Brooks. "I look for these players to play hard, to play smart and to represent their country."

This exciting semifinal game became known as the Miracle on Ice.

Team USA beat USSR 4 to 3 before going on to beat Finland for Gold.

In 2018 in PyeongChang the USA women's team won the Gold medal, beating Team Canada.

Pro Players

In 1998, Olympic hockey experienced a big change. For the first time, players from the National Hockey League were allowed to participate. The NHL includes many of the best hockey players in the world.

Fans loved it! You might have two teammates for the NHL's Detroit Red Wings play against each other, if one was from Canada and the other was from the United States. Or, you might have two players from rival NHL teams play on the same Olympic team, if they were both from the same country.

Women's hockey was added to the Winter Olympics in 1998. Canada had won four gold medals in a row until the United States won in 2018. It wasn't quite as surprising as the Miracle on Ice, but American hockey fans once again had reason to cheer.

USA's Monique Lamoureaux-Morando

BOBSLEIGH

USA 4-man bobsleigh competes in 2018.

There are three **traditional** sledding events at the Winter Games: luge, skeleton and bobsleigh.

In luge, athletes lie on their backs on a flat sled, and slide down the track feet first. In skeleton, the competitors lie on their stomachs on a similar sled and go down head first.

Anton Dukach of Ukraine competes in Singles Luge, 2018.

Bobsleigh is different from luge and skeleton in two major ways. First, the sled is bigger, with a front and two sides and a hole in the top for the athletes to get in and out of. And second, bobsleigh is a team sport! Four riders have to work together to go as fast as they can down the slippery track.

The 4-man bobsleigh team from Germany wins Gold in PyeongChang, 2018.

Bobsleigh was invented in Switzerland in the late 1860s. It was named because of the bobbing motion riders would use to steer the sled.

People had been riding on sleds across snow and ice for hundreds of years before that. But it wasn't until then that people starting using bigger sleds to carry multiple passengers.

When people added steering devices to their bobsleds, they could drive them down the hills of the town over long distances. But people who were walking around the town didn't like that either. Soon, there were bobsleds everywhere!

Around that same time, the town of St. Moritz, Switzerland, was becoming a popular gathering spot for people in the winter. People would come from all around to see the beautiful mountains. Sledding was a great way for them to pass the time! But there was one problem: They couldn't steer their sleds, so they kept running over people and into buildings!

St. Moritz bobsleigh run in 1905

The First Track

The owner of one of the best hotels in the town of St. Moritz didn't want people to get hurt. But he also didn't want people to stop bobsledding. So, in the 1870s, he opened the world's first bobsled track. The bobsledders loved it, and the people in the town could walk around safely again.

In no time at all, people were finding ways to have races on their sleds. The first known formal competition was held in 1884 on a track called Cresta Run. The track is still in use today, though it is now used for skeleton.

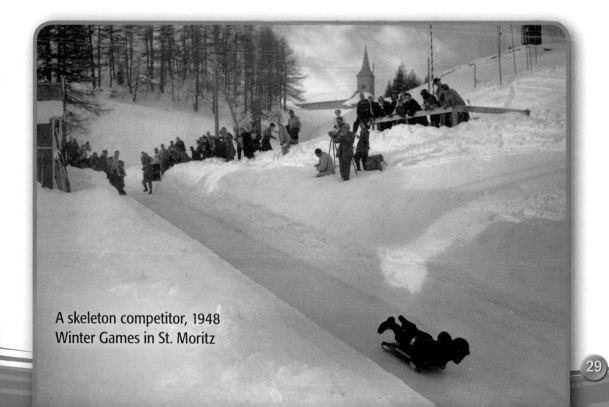

A skeleton competitor, 1948
Winter Games in St. Moritz

Bobsleigh is one of the most popular Winter Olympic team sports because the sleds go very fast. The winning team in the Olympics usually goes faster than 80 miles per hour (128 km/h).

It takes teamwork to go that fast. At the start of each run, the four athletes push their sled along the track as fast as they can. When they get close to the starting point, they have to jump in the sled one at time. Then they steer it down the track. It takes a lot of practice to get it just right.

Aerial view of a bobsleigh track.

Croatia's 4-man bobsleigh team competes in 2018.

The team from Great Britain in 2018, PyeongChang

Here Comes Jamaica!

One of the most famous winter sports teams out there is the Jamaican national bobsleigh team. In 1988, they made it to the Olympics for the first time. It was surprising because Jamaica is a **tropical** country. It never snows there!

The Jamaican team had almost no experience going down an icy track. At the Olympics, they had to borrow sleds from other countries. All of the other bobsleigh athletes were very friendly to the Jamaicans. They wanted to see them succeed.

Jamaica's 4-man bobsleigh team debuts at 1988 Games in Calgary.

Jamaica competed again in
two-man bobsleigh, Sochi, 2014.

Unfortunately, the Jamaican team crashed and did not get a medal. Still, everybody loved the Jamaican bobsleigh team. They even had a movie made about their experience.

The team would return to the Olympics to compete several more times.

CURLING

The women's curling team from South Korea won Silver in 2018.

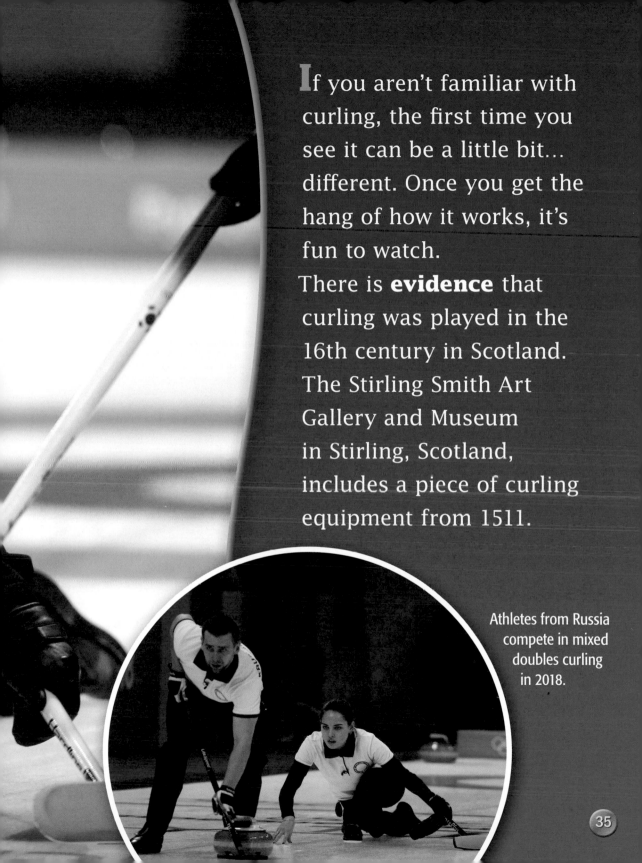

If you aren't familiar with curling, the first time you see it can be a little bit... different. Once you get the hang of how it works, it's fun to watch.

There is **evidence** that curling was played in the 16th century in Scotland. The Stirling Smith Art Gallery and Museum in Stirling, Scotland, includes a piece of curling equipment from 1511.

Athletes from Russia compete in mixed doubles curling in 2018.

35

Over the next few hundred years, the game gradually spread throughout the world. The Royal Montreal Curling Club in Canada was **established** in 1807 and is still active today.

But how exactly do you play curling? That's a **complicated** question. Curling teams have four players, and each of them has an important job to do.

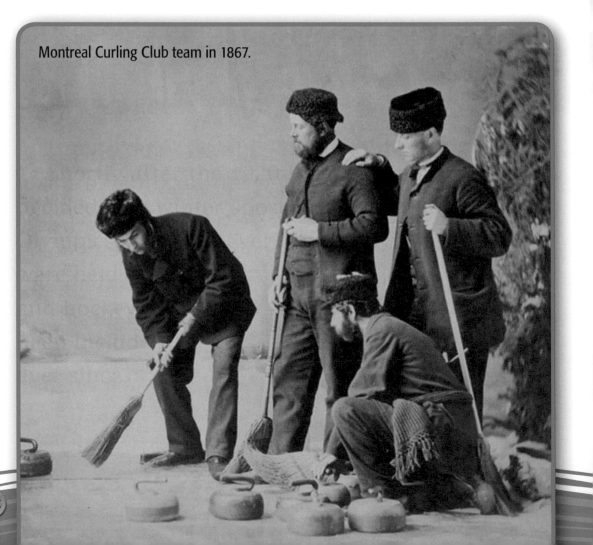

Montreal Curling Club team in 1867.

First, the "thrower" gets ready to go at one end of the playing area. The game begins when the thrower pushes a large, smooth rock called the "stone" down the ice. The stone **glides** all the way down to the other end. The players are not allowed to touch it once the thrower sends it on its way.

However, there is one special way that the thrower's teammates can control the stone.

Sweeping Up

Two players, called "sweepers," use brooms to help steer the stone in the right direction. But they still can't actually touch the stone. Instead, sweepers brush the ice in front of the stone to make it smoother so the stone will move faster.

As the stone slows down, it tends to **curl** in one direction or the other. (That's why they call it curling.) The sweepers can keep the stone moving straight ahead by sweeping more and more. Their arms must get tired!

2018 Curling medal winners: (L to R) Sweden wins Silver, USA wins Gold, Switzerland wins Bronze.

The fourth member of the team is called the "skip." The skip is the team **captain**. He or she decides how far the stone should go, and whether or not it should curl to a certain spot on the ice.

The skip will often shout out **commands** to his teammates while the stone is sliding down the ice. The skip will call the "line," or the direction he wants to the stone to go. The sweepers might call out the "weight," or the speed of the stone.

The skip is always watching the stone and deciding if it needs to go faster or slower, or if it needs to curl into the right position.

Great Britain's women's team competes in 2018.

What's the purpose of all of this throwing and sweeping? To score more points than the other team, of course!

At the opposite end of the ice from the thrower is a target, called the "house." It looks kind of like a target with a bull's eye that you would see in shooting sports, except it's painted flat on the ice. Curlers might try to make their stone curl so it stops right in the middle of the house.

To The House!

The purpose of the game is to get as many stones as possible as close as you can to the center of the house. But here's the problem: Every time one team finishes throwing a stone, the other team gets to throw one at the same house, too.

Sometimes it seems like one team is set up to score a lot of points, then all of a sudden the other team's stone will knock their stone out of the way. That's when curling gets really exciting. The skip has to decide if their team is going to try to get stones as close to the center of the house as possible, or if they're going to try to knock the other team's stones out of the way.

Whew! As you can tell, there are a lot of things going on in curling.

USA's Becca and Matt Hamilton compete in mixed doubles curling.

South Korea's women compete against the Gold medal team from Sweden, 2018.

Two USA athletes in
Pair Skating, 2018.

Team Figure Skating? Kind Of…

Olympics figure skating is mostly known as an individual sport. However, pair skating has been part of the Olympics as long as individual skating. Most people don't consider it to be a team sport, but pair skating does require two skaters to work together.

Pair skating involves one male and one female skater. Because there are two people on the ice, pair skaters can do things that individual skaters cannot. The most exciting pair skating moves are lifts, in which one skater lifts the other into the air. Sometimes one skater will even throw the other into the air! Just another example of a team of athletes working together.

Two French athletes in Team Pair Skating, 2018.

Germany's Gold-medal champs in Team Pair Skating

GLOSSARY

captain the person in charge

challenge something that is very difficult

chant when a large group of people yell the same words at the same time

command orders or instructions

complicated something that is difficult or confusing

continent a giant piece of land that might include more than one country

curl a curved shape

develop to come up with an idea

discussion a talk between people who are trying to come to a decision

dominate to be far and away the best at a sport

establish when something is set up for the first time

evidence facts that indicate that something is true

glide to move across something with a smooth motion

international something that happens between two or more countries

modern something that happened recently

organizers people who plan an event

rally when a sports team is losing but still trying to come back and win

reconsider to think more about something

steer to control the direction of something

track a course made for a sports competition

traditional something that has been going on for a long time

tropical a place where it's always warm

FOR MORE INFORMATION

Books

Burgen, Michael. *Miracle on Ice: How a Stunning Upset United a Country*. Compass Point, 2016.

Coffey, Wayne. *The Boys of Winter: The Untold Story of a Coach, a Dream, and the 1980 U.S. Olympic Hockey Team*. Crown Publishers. 2005.

Harris, Devon. *Yes, I Can! The Story of the Jamaican Bobsled Team*. Waterhouse Publishing. 2008.

Waxman, Laura Hamilton. *Ice Hockey and Curling (Winter Olympic Sports series)*. Amicus, 2017.

Places

Lake Placid Olympic Training Center, Lake Placid, New York. U.S. Olympic Training Center, and host of the 1932 and 1980 Winter Games.

Utah Olympic Park, Park City, Utah. Winter sports park built for the 2002 Winter Olympics.

Squaw Valley Ski Resort, Placer County, California. Host site of the 1960 Winter Olympics.

INDEX

ABOUT THE AUTHOR

Aaron Derr is a writer based just outside of Dallas, Texas. He has more than 15 years of experience as a writer and editor for magazines such as *Sports Illustrated for Kids*, *TIME for Kids*, and *Boys Life*. When he's not reading or writing, Aaron enjoys watching and playing sports, and doing pretty much anything with his wife and two kids.